AROMA
OF A
REBEL

CAPTAIN ROBERT BAILEY

First published by Pibly 2012

978-0-9538620-3-0

DEDICATION

To my family and friends

CONTENTS

DIY

ACKNOWLEDGMENTS

My daughter Pesha (Pat Bailey) for making this book possible

1 OLD LANCASHIRE JOKE

Bob and Jack were returning,

They'd been on the bevy all night,

Their quickest way home, was the churchyard,

Though the night wasn't too bright.

Then Bob found that he was walking

And Jack wasn't there by his side,

He thought, where is Jack, I'd better turn back.

And came to a grave, open wide.

He tried to look down in the darkness,

Couldn't lean too far for the beer,

Although rather low, a voice from below,

Said it's ruddy cold down here.

So Bob started side footing soil in,

Still struggling with his hiccup,

No wonder that thar't feelin cowd bad,

Nobody's covered thee up.

2 QUEEN'S TROOPING THE COLOUR IN HER JUBILEE YEAR 1977

How wonderful this pageant,

We watch on BBC,

The Queen in all her glory,

For all the world to see.

The worldwide famous British Guards,

On this day queenly led,

Her uniform to match the troops,

In black and vivid red.

To hear the British Grenadiers,

The wearing of the Green,

Behind the bagpiped Highlander,

The Welsh Guards can be seen.

The massed bands playing on the march,

The guards with measured tread,

The cream of Scottish, Irish, Welsh,

With Coldstreams at their head.

How these old shoulders straightened,

To hear these martial airs,

Though nearly forty years have passed,

Yet still the old blood stirs.

That six o'clock reveille,

Then out of Nissen hut,

The rifle slope then ordered,

Presented, slap the butt.

The Queen inspects with regal air,

Her standard now unfurled,

Five hundred million see our Queen,

The envy of the world.

All these old memories can't detract

From this parade today.

What other country in the world

Can show this royal way?

With millions of old soldiers,

How proud the day is made,

Salute the Duke of Lancaster,

The Queen is on parade.

I wrote a copy of this poem to Her Majesty at Buckingham Palace and was delighted to receive a reply which read

Dear Mr Bailey,

I'm commanded by the Queen to thank you for the poem which you have written on the occasion of the Trooping the Colour. The Queen much enjoyed reading it and thought it was kind of you to send it to her.

Yours sincerely,

3 QUEEN'S JUBILEE: ALSO THE WRITER'S BIRTHDAY 7 JUNE 1977

Such pageantry can be so clear

On coloured BBC.

The miracle that colour brings,

The Queen's own Jubilee.

The Queen in matching hat and coat,

A lovely shade of pink,

And women viewing everywhere

Are too entranced to blink.

But who with such a regal air

Could wear such sunshine yellow?

Except the Mother Queen so fair

Whose years have left so mellow.

The gold coach stops at Temple Bar.

The Mayor, with keys in hand,

Now London's gates are opened to

Our Lady of this land.

Who can describe such coloured scene,

With viewers by the million,

Six Windsor greys, on shortened rein,

Outriders and *postillion.

The Queen in coach, the Prince behind.

Our lovely Queen all smiles.

The greatest country and its Queen,

These lovely British Isles.

*A postillion was a rider and driver on one of the horses which pulled a carriage. He would usually ride on the left or nearside horse.

4 OPPOSITION TO STRIKERS

Let's all feel sorry for't strikers,

Who only earn ninety or more.

Except when they've gone two days absent,

Then it's around sixty four.

They won't call a strike till it's freezing,

They kill hundreds more when it's cold.

The main ones to die will be children,

Or geezers like me, getting old.

The children die, burning and screaming,

A candle set fire to the bed.

Perhaps it's a paraffin heater,

But the children are still just   as dead.

AROMA OF A REBEL

The doctor say hypo-ther-mia,

The Coroner's inquest is told.

I don't know hypo-ther-mia,

All I know, me feet's getting cold.

The strikers say they work in danger,

Conditions not fit for a dog.

But my mate a long distance driver,

Just got himself killed in the fog.

Another mate sailed out of Fleetwood,

He knew just how cold it could get.

He didn't mind this, until one day,

He went overboard with the net.

A neighbour's son read all the adverts,

Professional Army career.

Inside of two years he's in action,

We went to his funeral this year.

CAPTAIN ROBERT BAILEY

With millions of British old soldiers,

We fought without grumbling too much.

So all English children, including strikers,

Could grow up without speaking Deutche.

And now we get our old age pension,

Which doesn't go far I confess.

Or else on the dole, no free issues at all,

And the strikers couldn't care less.

Just hark at the brass effrontery

Of some of our national MP's.

Yelling resign for the public good,

When the public's all people like me.

I don't even know where they come from,

But there's just one thing, I must say,

We've got queer ideas, in Lancashire,

Like wanting to see some fair play.

AROMA OF A REBEL

We'll listen to all their opinions,

But when they're finished and done.

They're only one man among millions

Entitled to their bit of fun.

Someone should tell them the story

Of Roses match at Headingley.

The neutral spectator was very soon told,

Look lad, there's nowt here for thee.

So please Mr. MP for Somewhere,

We've read all thy speeches and laughed.

We might be a bit cabbage- looking

But don't think we're all ruddy daft.

5 EFFORTS IN POETRY

After weeks of nauseating news of Harold Wilson and his honours list, I decided that a real old fashioned Valentine would make better reading. Surprisingly, the local paper, our Blackpool Gazette, printed it.

Oh how it makes my heart rejoice,

To hear that lovely smiling voice.

The day's gloom lifter every time,

O would'st thou be my Valentine?

This eye rewarding, moving grace,

As lovely patterned silken lace.

The swan-like neck of Doric line,

O maketh me thy Valentine.

AROMA OF A REBEL

But all this surface beauty shown,

Enrobes a nature all its own.

Reflecting free from eyes that shine,

I'll die, were not thy Valentine.

So sweetest maid, please spare a glance,

As ladies old at guerdoned lance.

Command this knight thy right divine,

As lifelong champion Valentine.

.

6 ANOTHER VALENTINE

This bleeding heart with oft spent sighs,

At one glance from those lovely eyes,

Would cupid's arrow ease the pain?

Could I but earn one glance again?

Alas this Goddess does not know,

How love like mine gives heartfelt glow.

How tremulous this beating heart:

Such lovely pain from cupid's dart.

AROMA OF A REBEL

How can I say my maiden fair,

Of lovely eyes and golden hair.

That this poor mortal heart a pine,

Would'st hope to be thy Valentine.

Such flawless beauty textured fine,

As mermaids, sylph-like lovely line.

My bursting heart, my all is thine.

Could I but be thy Valentine?

7 AN AGE-OLD VALENTINE AFTER 40 YEARS OF MARRIAGE

Tho' neither tall, handsome and fair,

And time has bleached his once dark hair,

For countless years this man of mine,

Has always been my Valentine.

From careless youth with sparkling eye,

Young springy step and marriage nigh.

How can the years pass by so quick?

Now wryly asks "where is my stick?"

AROMA OF A REBEL

The awful parting in the War,

Now time goes slowly from afar.

But back he came, oh lovely time,

For all these years my Valentine.

How to express what this has meant,

With happy heart of sweet content.

A lovely lifetime, set to rhyme,

How thankful for my Valentine.

8 ANOTHER VALENTINE: A DIFFERENT YEAR

Oh lovely maid, so sweet of face,

Slim figured line, such lissom grace.

All nature's best in natural line,

My dearest wish, thy Valentine.

Were I so bold, my lovely star,

Sweet maid tho' worshipped from afar.

Would love for thee so hopeless be?

Could I tell thee my heart's in fee?

AROMA OF A REBEL

O that we lived in days of old,

With chivalry to help the bold.

No deed's too much for thee, my sweet,

My heart and sword both at thy feet.

*Caparisoned horse with hooves a dance,

Thy scarf the guerdon on my lance.

No dragons safe in all this time,

For thee my lovely Valentine.

So please sweet maid, use lovely eyes,

To find thy knight of heartfelt sighs.

This heart is thine, for more than time,

Thy lifelong love, thy Valentine.

- Caparisoned horse is a riderless horse with boots reversed in the stirrup used in processions. It symbolizes where the rider can ride no more.

9 VALENTINE TO BRITISH LEYLAND

How can it feel this heart so weak?

I've only know her for one week.

So beautiful of lovely line,

My week old, secret Valentine.

Then, when I take her down the street,

How envious the men I meet.

The moving curtains pushed aside,

My heart brims o'er with loving pride.

AROMA OF A REBEL

How to describe such moving grace,

Descendant of a graceful race.

This air that pedigree has wrought,

No wonder that my heart was caught.

My thoughts are full of her at night,

Such lovely dreams, my heart is light.

How I look forward to the dawn,

Each morning's sight, new love is born.

The garden glows, my heart's alive,

To see her standing in the drive.

No other could outshine a star,

My British Leyland MG car.

.

10 TAKING A DOG A WALK

A lady wrote to the local paper saying that, taking a friend's dog for a walk in Stanley Park, she was horrified to find the Park's Department men cutting down the trees.

My reply was not printed by the Gazette.

My dear Miss Smith I sympathise

To read the awful fact

About the men at Stanley Park

Who wield such ruthless axe.

To take a friend's dog for a walk

In Blackpool's balmy breeze,

Arrive at Stanley Park to find,

They're cutting down the trees.

AROMA OF A REBEL

But never mind my dear Miss Smith,

The thing that matters most.

You'll find that to and from the Park,

There's always some lamp posts.

11 MURDER OF CHRISTOPHER MCDONALD: MAY 14TH 1978 NEWS

A young policeman called Christopher McDonald, nineteen years old, was found murdered in a canal. It was presumed he was chasing crooks, when he met his death. It was later found he had been chasing a burglar in Worksop who had been robbing a jewellers He was killed with is own truncheon and a brick. His murderer was later convicted. At nineteen years old, he was just a boy, doing a man's work.

How is it possible to me, at seventy years old, to imagine life so far back as nineteen years old?

Chris McDonald died today,

Never heard of him you say.

He was just nineteen years old,

Now he's lying stiff and cold.

AROMA OF A REBEL

Whilst we were in our beds asleep

He walked his lonely midnight beat.

Far too courageous for his years.

Such courage brings a mother's tears.

It's no use talking policeman's pay,

He cannot hear a word you say.

No wife or children to enjoy.

He died, and only just a boy.

How can you measure man's estate,

When boys surpass their elders' state?

We take for granted what they do

Because their uniform is blue.

How can we judge a boy so fine,

Who lays his life upon the line?

He only thinks his duty's due,

Because policemen always do.

CAPTAIN ROBERT BAILEY

And so to Chris this tribute true,

No words can make it up to you.

Your love one's pride, they know you died,

Because your uniform was blue.

12 BURTON'S SALE AT TOWN HALL

In April 1977 Messrs Burton the Tailors had a clear out sale at the local town hall.

The local shopkeepers were furious the Town Hall could be used for a one day sale, especially for the civil servants.

The Town Clerk assured us the only sale took place outside working hours. This was in reply to an angry letter from the Secretary from the local Chamber of Trade.

We never know what we will read

When we buy our Gazette.

Some funny things, peculiar,

But here's the best one yet.

CAPTAIN ROBERT BAILEY

On April 21st, we read,

That in our own Town Hall.

The Burtons clear outs were so cheap,

The staff had quite a ball.

Like Caesar's wife they can't do wrong,

Don't have to toe the line.

Like Mayoral car, that stood all day,

On double yellow lines.

The sale was in non-working hours,

To hear the Town Clerk speak,

And naïve ratepayers believe

His tongue's not in his cheek.

The NALGO staffroom was the shop,

With racks and racks of clothes.

With Mayor's parlour coyly placed

For trying pantyhose.

AROMA OF A REBEL

Chamber of Trade, with hackled back,

Objects, says Mr Knowles,

We'll put the Town Clerk on the rack,

Instead of all these clothes.

Not for today the gavels sound,

But this I'd love to see.

And hear the Town Clerk's dulcet tones,

*"Mayor Hudson - are you free?"

Line adapted from a well known comedy "Are you being served"

.

13 SPRING

The morning paper's just arrived,

The news always depressing,

And then the garden meets the eye,

The antidote refreshing.

Here's April, such a lovely month,

It brings such lovely things.

Winter's darkness now is past,

Birds mating, call it Spring.

The rosebush, apple, try their green,

To vie with nesting bird.

The daffodils are at their best,

And then the cuckoo's heard.

So Doctor Owen's in S.A.

Who cares what news he brings.

There's lovely sunshine just outside,

This miracle called Spring.

*A cherry tree from planted stone,

Its blossom covered white.

The almond's bloom is not alone,

In showing Nature's night.

All this is prompted by today,

A day that won't be marred.

The smiling postman's hand is filled,

You've guessed, they're Birthday cards.

*This cherry tree is still blossoming and producing fruit 35 years later.

14 MIND WANDERING

Now Mary had a little lamb,

And ee, it were a good 'un.

It never wanted out to eat,

Because it were a wood'un.

15 DAD'S NEW WHEELCHAIR

Dad eyed the wheelchair up and down,

And said, it's new to me.

I've driven cars for fifty years,

I'll drive this too, you'll see.

He settled down upon the seat,

And hitched up both his braces.

Grabbed the handrims on the wheels,

And said, I'm going places.

So when you're strolling on the prom,

You'll know Dad's got the knack.

He's got an L plate on his chest,

Another on his back.

With this wheelchair, I'll start a band,

Three piece with Tom and Pat.

I'm mobile now that I'm on wheels,

My walking stick - old hat.

Tom has the big drum on his knee,

He plays by rule of thumb.

Enthusiasm lent him strength,

He'd bust the raucous drum.

Patrick plays the old trombone,

A sailor old, he led.

And what a sight to see these three

Wheelchairs, in line ahead.

So when arthritis pains your joints,

Get rid of walking sticks.

With wheelchair you can join our band,

Called Jerry and his Jerry Hat Tricks.

16 CHRISTMAS CARD PRICE

The shock of buying a Christmas card, then discovering the price.

I chose the Christmas cards I like,

Then took them to the till.

But when the man told me the price,

My beating heart stood still.

My voice tried hard to make a noise.

Impossible to clear.

The man had rung upon his till,

Before I said, "too dear."

CAPTAIN ROBERT BAILEY

So now you see no words inside,

I feel it is my duty,

To leave the card in lovely white,

Nor mar its virgin beauty.

Another reason is my mind,

Which never analysed,

The shock's affected writing arm,

And left it paralysed.

.

17 ON SPENDING A SUMMER'S DAY

The Spanish fisherman knew best,

When in the Summer heat,

Refused the tourists hire of boat,

Said "Senor, it's not treat.

The Good Lord sent this lovely day,

His children to enjoy.

I work for almost all the year,

And holidays abhor.

So why should I, this lovely day,

Hire out my boat to fish,

When I can be here in the shade,

Siesta is my wish."

18 LANCASHIRE COUNTY PALATINE: QUEEN'S JUBILEE 1977

Now in this lovely country,

Composed of many shires,

There is one special county,

We call it Lancashire.

Now why should it be different,

In England's lovely scene?

Because this special Duchy's

Ennobled by the Queen.

Since the day of John O'Gaunt,

Who lived in Ancient time.

Our ruling monarch has been Duke,

AROMA OF A REBEL

Of County Palatine.

The many titles of the Queen,

All honourable estate.

Though deeply steeped in history,

To us are not so great.

As when we drink the loyal toast,

In pub or regiment.

We toast the Duke of Lancaster,

And all know who is meant.

There's fifty million people,

Live in this pleasant land,

But none so fiercely loyal,

As Lancashire's own band.

There's forty million subjects

Who toast "Our Queen" and look,

Ten million more in Lancashire,

Will toast our special Duke.

That's why all over Lancashire,

Where 'ere you go. you'll see

There's flags up by the thousand,

Our own Duke's Jubilee.

19 NEW HOUSING ESTATE

A new housing estate was built and newcomers objected to the numerous cars which parked near a well known ice cream parlour.

This prompted the following poem 21.7.1977

Some folk are so peculiar,

The blame is never theirs.

They always blame the other man,

Right through the passing years.

My mate, he bought himself a house,

With furniture, as well.

He bought it near the gas works,

Now, objects to the smell.

CAPTAIN ROBERT BAILEY

The gasworks been there fifty years,

His house is not yet proved.

He's written counsellors, MPs.

He wants the gasworks moved.

Another mate, he bought a house,

Next door to a farm.

He talked about the rural life,

In it he saw no harm.

But this first year of muck spreading,

He ranted and he fumed.

I've got to get this farmer moved,

Cos' all is pig perfumed.

My Fleetwood mate who bought his house,

Right near to't glue factory,

Has written Walter Clegg MP

This bad olfactory.

The moral of this lesson is,

Don't buy a house, then scream

The agent never told me that,

It's near a hideous dream.

20 THE WOULD BE CHICKEN FARMER

He bought one thousand day old chicks,

Next day a thousand more,

A thousand on the third day,

But the breeder said, no more.

Your land is far too small,

These birds, you'll never rear,

You're thinking then, the buyer said,

I'm planting them too near?

21 PATRICIA'S BIRTHDAY 1978

This coincided with my heart attack which did not help the celebration.

I'm always sure that Daddy

Will think of something new.

As always on my birthday,

There's no-one feeling blue.

But this year is the limit,

There's nothing that we lack,

It's really going much too far,

To have a heart attack.

With normal entertainment,

All that we understand,

A heart attack's ridiculous,

A thing we don't demand

So let's get back to normal,

Good wishes by the score,

And for our lovely daughter,

Good health for evermore.

22 SHOCKING KETTLE

Today my wife received an electric shock using a patented switching-off kettle. We found (later) water had penetrated the automatic switch causing a short, which made the kettle live.

My wife picked up the kettle to make tea, received a severe shock, fortunately she was able to drop the kettle and rush into the lounge. Unbelievably, it was days before the shock wore off. The moral being, always pull out the wall plug before using an electric kettle. The pain, over days moved around various parts of her body which was disconcerting.

Today she doesn't feel too well,

Not in the best of fettle.

She gets a pain that moves around,

All from that shocking kettle.

The pain it moves from here to there,

It doesn't like to settle,

All because of water in,

That stupid, shocking kettle.

She rubs the pain that's in her arm,

Then suddenly it goes.

Before she know what else to rub,

She finds it in her toes.

All this was caused, electric shock,

We don't know how it feels.

But moving pain like this must cause,

From two electric heels.

Now my wife won't take a chance,

Tho' making tea time jellies.

She'll only put the kettle on

In rubber gloves and wellies.

23 MUSHY PEAS

This little poem, published in the Women's section of the Evening Gazette, created a lot of interest.

Dear Editor, a cri de Coeur

To set my mind at ease.

In spite of different ways I've tried,

I can't cook mushy peas.

Potatoes boiled and baked, croquettes,

With cauliflower cheese.

Delicious carrots, buttered, mashed,

But never mushy peas.

I've soaked them overnight to swell,

I've tried from pod and tin.

But when I get them in the pan,

The peas won't just give in.

I've boiled them short; I've boiled them long,

With gas both high and low,

The net results don't justify

A satisfying glow.

I bring them out with hopes set high

And serve them piping hot.

Alas they roll about the plate

Like number ten lead shot.

There must be thousands more like me

Whose yearning so to please.

And search the culinary heights

Of serving mushy peas.

To all the chaps in Blackpool then,

I send this heartfelt plea.

What do I have to do to get

A green and mushy pea?

24 THANK YOU TO MUSHY PEAS REPLY

The reply from the Gazette about Mushy Peas inspired a thank you.

How kindly are the ladies

Who all read our Gazette.

Read my plea for mushy peas.

The telephone rings yet.

I'd like to thank these ladies,

None of whom I've met.

And all of Women's Circle,

Our page in the Gazette.

AROMA OF A REBEL

The recipes contagious,

I started the next day.

The work enthusiastic,

Success came straight away.

With trembling hands, I served them,

Exalted, rosy face,

Each portion without movement:

They all stayed on one place.

The family cheers still echo,

The most I've had for years.

They've only one complaint to make,

They've peas coming out their ears.

25 REPLY TO MUSHY PEAS RECIPE FROM MRS CLARKSON

Mushy peas recipe received from Mrs Clarkson Cleveleys January 12 1982

My dear Mrs Clarkson, how nice,

No words of mine can suffice

To thank you enough, you do know your stuff,

I've just read your recipe twice.

It must be a kindly nature,

To take all the trouble to write

To me a perfect stranger

Who cannot get mushy peas right.

AROMA OF A REBEL

So clear are your instructions,

Even I couldn't help get it right.

Adverts that state success on a plate,

Just proved your instructions are right.

And so, my dear Mrs Clarkson,

My choice of the chefs of all ranks.

I write you a personal poem,

To express my most fervent thanks.

May this year for you be a blessing,

Achieving all that you please.

And bringing this from one grateful family

Who now can cook nice mushy peas.

.

26 REPLY TO MRS SHAW FOR MUSHY PEAS RECIPE

My dear Mrs Shaw, how delightful

To read of those earlier times

When naval men went into forage

And plunder the marrow fat mines

In those days, when we had an Empire,

The Navy was always at ease;

And *matelots took it for granted

They'd always get their mushy peas.

AROMA OF A REBEL

With intrepid chefs on the ramparts,

The foraging party was sure

To do all they could to show *Nelson's blood

To bring back the mushy peas lure.

So landlubbers all over England

Give thanks to our Naval lads please,

Who all in old times charged the marrowfat mines

To bring back our nice mushy peas.

* matelot is a sailor

*Nelson Blood is Naval rum issue.

27 SNOW JANUARY/FEBRUARY 1984

This morning I'm feeling lighthearted,

Wonderfully cheerful and fit.

In spite of the cold, I'm not feeling old,

My family say, pushing a bit.

It started when I saw the garden,

Some snow that had gone overnight,

And there in its place, in front of my face,

A marvel of Nature's delight.

To see what a nice interruption,

To all of our everyday toil.

In spite of the gales, blizzard and hail,

Green shoots pushing up through the soil.

AROMA OF A REBEL

Forgetting housewife's aggravation,

The electric kettle won't boil,

The toaster won't work, the weather's berserk,

And the man says the Hoover needs oil.

Who cares for these tribulations?

There's nothing that this day can spoil.

I feel I must write, of this lovely sight,

Green shoots pushing up through the soil.

And that's why I've this lovely feeling,

In spite of the winter's large bills.

I know in my heart, with this lovely start,

We're promised our spring daffodils.

So lets all say goodbye to winter,

And think what the New Year can bring.

Forget all the snow, with Nature aglow,

This wonderful time we call Spring.

28 SARAH

Owld Sarah's on her death bed,

Twas plain far aw to see,

Her face was whitish lukkin,

Her's nobbut ninety three.

Owd Tom sai, "Na then Sarah,

Ah know tha weren't be hurried,

Ah've allus done mi best for Thee,

Naow where would'e like to be buried?"

Owld Sarah sat up sharply,

Th'owd glint were in her ee,

"Ah've allus had one place picked aet,

And that's on't top o' Thee."

29 FUNERAL PARLOUR IN QUEEN STREET

In the Blackpool Gazette was an announcement a church building in Queen Street was to be demolished. The land offered for sale had been purchased by a local firm of undertakers.

We always think things could be worse,

That's why I feel this sudden verse.

I wonder if you've missed the news

About the land that once held pews.

A businessman who bought the land,

He wants his business to expand,

Not selling silks, or panty hose,

But build a Chapel of Repose.

Where once we heard the Preacher say,

"How short is life, and but one way."

So fitting that this new retreat

Be built upon a one way street.

One hundred yards from Mothercare,

How quick the journey, starting there,

Old adage, and the time we save,

How quick from cradle to the grave.

How straight the line, for *Layton bound,

There's just the Odeon to get round.

Unless a moratorium,

For Carleton crematorium.

The visitor will stand and stare,

Just look what's on that corner there,

A bucket now won't make the grade,

I'll have to buy a bigger spade.

AROMA OF A REBEL

And when our ladies brave the gales

For Queen Street's bargain Winter Sales,

Don't say this bargain's best by far

Because you've got a hatch back car.

*Layton is a local cemetery.

30 IN APPRECIATION – A PRESENT FOR ANY MOTHER

There's no time like the present,

When you're not feeling well,

To get a little parcel,

Your head clears like a bell.

A present for the present,

It's just an in-between.

Not birthday or for Christmas,

But just so you'll have seen.

AROMA OF A REBEL

It's here because we love you,

We don't need more excuse.

We're maybe almost helpless,

But prove we have some use.

If only now to show you,

The sympathy we share,

And hope you'll soon be feeling well,

The present's on your chair.

31 SUPERMARKETS WRITTEN JANUARY 1986

I'm just a hardworking housewife,

My height just five foot three.

But the shelves in our supermarket,

Are obviously not meant for me.

My troubles start with the trolley,

The moment I look up, I find,

Three wheels will always go one way,

And the other can't make up its mind.

Along with all other housewives,

The trolleys, like ships line ahead.

AROMA OF A REBEL

I enjoy the sport, I turn hard port,

But the darn thing goes starboard instead.

But yesterday brought near disaster,

I tried to reach the top shelf.

I fumbled a tin, which then fell in,

I've no-one to blame but myself.

I hadn't seen this little doggie

In front of me on the floor.

Though I tried to help, he gave a loud yelp,

And made a bee line for the door.

His paw made four little skid marks,

He took off and knocked down some bread.

As I told my Bert, who wouldn't feel hurt,

When a pound tin dropped on your head.

He skidded when turning the corner,

His owner shot out of her jeans.

His rear end came round, tail close to the ground,

And knocked down the pyramid beans.

In front of a very fat lady,

Had just started turning around.

He caught her wrong angle, his lead was entangled,

She sat with a bump on the ground.

I could tell she didn't like doggies,

When she shouted at him from the floor.

She even knew his antecedents

Though she hadn't seen him before.

The dog leapt away to the checkout,

Still wearing a fat lady's hat.

And a man said, "By gum,

He's good as *Red Rum."

The check out girl said, "what was that?"

The moral of this little story

Is obvious now to you all,

Don't have any part of your supermart

Unless you're at least six foot tall.

*Red Rum was a racehorse who won the Grand National in 1973, 1974 and 1977 and came second in the intervening years.

32 A NEIGHBOUR'S BIRTHDAY 28TH MARCH

O what a lovely day to-day,

Away from work can Muriel stay.

Instead of looking drawn and beat up,

She's on the settee, with her feet up.

Not polishing around the chairs

Or running up and downstairs.

Back garden chair to get suntanned

A glass of "birthdays" in her hand.

AROMA OF A REBEL

So our lovely Muriel,

We send out love and wish her well,

For all the future coming years,

All love and joy, and no more tears.

33 SEAT BELTS

This new law for the safety belt,

Against the old is mostly felt.

This strap of hard spun cotton weave

Makes it most difficult to breathe.

There's just one way, Police to fool,

A Doctor can by-pass the rule.

Alas, alack, and woe is me,

For this, the Doctor wants a fee.

34 VALENTINE TO THE LADY TRAFFIC WARDEN

One of the worst sights in the Land

To see that hat with yellow band.

The figure short, so square and fat,

Who's ever send a Valentine to that?

In England here, the land of cricket,

The yellow band's like a sticky wicket.

It's just not done when you see the ticket

To tell the warden where to stick it.

35 VALENTINE

O lovely lady, dear to me,

Can words describe my love for thee?

That lovely face and sylph-like form,

Bright sunshine on a spring like morn.

How to describe that lovely face,

Where time has left no masking trace.

Reflecting too, a nature fine,

Who would not be thy Valentine?

And so my love, why can't I be

A suppliant for love of thee.

Devotion promised for all time,

If I can be thy Valentine.

36 VALENTINE FROM AUSTRALIA

Dear Marguerite of English charms,

Could I but take thee in my arms?

To hold this vision, lovely line,

And now I am thy Valentine.

Alas, this heart beats every day

For thee, ten thousand miles away.

Could miracled winged horse appear,

Transporting me to one so dear.

CAPTAIN ROBERT BAILEY

Winged Pegasus would never tire,

With love, a stallion shook with fire,

His arrowed course, with love like mine,

To carry thee my Valentine.

To Marguerite, my love, my rose,

My summer scented dahlia,

Who else could fill a heart, so far

Away, as South Australia.

And so, sweet maiden think of me,

My aching heart, so full of thee.

Proof positive to show I care,

I send my favourite Koala bear.

37 VALENTINE TO A LOVELY WIFE

Adventur'd day begins each morn,

How else could smiling face adorn.

Such lovely beauty, easy grace,

Surmounted by that lovely face.

No wonder, that my love, my all,

Love's prisoner that held in thrall.

That lovely picture, beauteous line,

My captive heart, thy Valentine.

No matter that the day is dull,

My heart is always overfull.

The dullness clears in graceful style,

At one glimpse of thy lovely smile.

And so, sweet maid, please spare a thought

At havoc that thy smile has wrought.

My overburdened heart is thine,

Could I but be thy Valentine?

Where else can love, with bursting heart,

That gives each day such lovely start.

My lovely maid, my life, my sweet,

My loving heart lies at thy feet.

38 OLD FASHIONED VALENTINE

O how it makes my heart rejoice

To hear that lovely smiling voice.

The day's gloom lifted every time,

O would'st thou be my Valentine?

Those features fair, that lovely face,

The figure slim, each movement's grace.

Bewitching eyes, 'neath eyebrow fine,

O wilt thou be my Valentine?

This eye rewarding, moving grace

As lovely patterned, silken lace.

The swan-like neck, of Doric line.

O maketh me thy Valentine.

But all this surface beauty shown

Enrobes a nature, all its own.

Reflecting free, from eyes that shine,

I'll die were not thy Valentine.

So sweetest maid, please spare a glance

As ladies old, at guerdon'd lance,

Command this knight, thy right divine,

As lifelong, charming Valentine.

39 VIP'S CLOAKROOM

Walking in Blackpool's Winter garden I was approached by a couple who asked me, "Where is the VIP's cloakroom?

Why people think that they

Are so important anyway?

They find themselves upon the earth

By sheer accident of birth.

As Shakespeare said, the pulling child

No choice that he, born high or wild,

His fate decided months ago,

To be born high or humble low.

CAPTAIN ROBERT BAILEY

How lucky he, who knows not need,

Was born from high contented seed.

His mother rates a second look

Because she's married to a Duke.

40 A CHRISTMAS CAROL

One lone star bright that lovely night,

That came before the dawn,

Illuminating Bethlehem

When Jesus Christ was born

Three wise men the stable mean,

A lantern on the chair.

Who'd know that man's salvation then

Was lying cradled there.

CAPTAIN ROBERT BAILEY

So all will know on Christmas day

That Jesus came from high.

So man could live for evermore

And mankind never die.

And so Believers on this earth

Combine as one to say

The greatest sacrifice of all

Was made for Christmas Day.

41 SAM'S LYING IN STATE

Owd Sam just kicked the bucket,

He were lying in state in't front room.

All the neighbours, paying respects,

Were sitting about in the gloom.

Then one of the neighbours consoling,

We'll do whatever we can.

I've never seen Sam looking better,

He was always a good looking man.

The widow then stopped her soft crying,

With pride her heart starts to swell.

We've just had our *Wakes week in Blackpool,

No wonder he's looking so well.

*Closing of all cotton mills in a town the same week and traditionally the workers went to Blackpool, a seaside town, for their holidays.

42 THE TURKEY BREEDER

For years he'd been breeding his turkeys,

A nice special breed, short and fat.

The breasts and the drumsticks world famous,

And you cannot do better than that.

A brilliant idea for more drumsticks,

If he could develop fresh eggs.

He'd get double the number of drumsticks

With turkeys that bred with four legs.

CAPTAIN ROBERT BAILEY

His friends said, what do they taste like?

With ordinary ones, can you match them?

He said, without haste, I don't know the taste,

They're running so fast, I can't catch them.

43 GRANDMA'S BIRTHDAY

A new twist on the old Australian convict story.

It was Grandma's sixtieth birthday,

She'd lived all her life here in Perth,

Second generation Australian,

Australians know what that's worth.

The family all gathered around her,

They sang "Happy Birthday" aloud.

Grandma was happy and glowing,

She looked at them all feeling proud.

The family said, well now, Grandma,

For a birthday present surprise,

The family have all clubbed together

To buy you a present travelwise.

For three moths a visit to England,

Taking one of the girls,

To see all the sights made world famous,

As the British landscape unfurls.

The sentries at Buckingham Palace,

More wonderful sights by the hour.

Illuminations at Blackpool,

Those colourful sights by the Tower.

But Grandma was looking quite worried,

She'd heard them called Pommies or Pom.

I'm not so sure about England,

Isn't that where the convicts came from?

44 SAM'S SAMPLE

Owd Sam arrived with his sample

At the surgery of Doctor McDowell,

Carrying a well known object,

Lightly disguised by a towel.

The doctor looked in astonishment,

He'd never had such a surprise.

You've never walked through the streets like that?

He couldn't believe his eyes.

It was Sam's turn to look astonished,

What do you think I am?

I wouldn't walk through the streets like this.

I got here o't top ot'h tram.

45 THE JOURNALIST

A journalist convalescent,

Ensconced in a country hotel.

The doctor said diet, and then country quiet,

And then we'll soon have you well.

He'd get up and started the morning,

A walk to the top of the hill,

And then looking back, this journalist hack,

On a country scene so nice and still.

CAPTAIN ROBERT BAILEY

He wrote that everything's peaceful,

An unusual honorarium.

The only signs of life I can see

Is the smoke from the town's crematorium.

46 ANOTHER CHRISTMAS CAROL

This miracle throughout the years,

When all the church bells ring

To celebrate the birth of Christ

And joyous Christians sing.

Two thousand years ago that night,

In far off Bethlehem,

The tired couple resting there,

A man-child born to them

CAPTAIN ROBERT BAILEY

No royal trumpets for this birth,

A stable old and worn,

A straw lined manger for a bed,

When Jesus Christ was born.

The wise men led by one bright star,

Not knowing how or where.

But bearing gifts of royal gold

With frankincense and myrrh.

So mankind upon this earth,

To all of rich and poor,

Because of Christmas long ago

Shall live for evermore.

47 A VALENTINE TO A HUSBAND

No film star he, with slicked back hair,

He's happy in his easy chair.

For forty years, this man of mine

Has always been my Valentine.

Not tall, his figure goes around,

Nor climbs the stairs in easy bounds.

He loves to have a little booze,

Then easy chair and gentle snooze.

But little glimpses, in between,

Disclose the man he's always been.

Through wear and tear, effects of time,

He'll always be my Valentine.

48 VALENTINE RECEIVED BY A HUSBAND

O what a beautiful surprise,

The postman shows my tired eyes.

That advanced age can blot out time

When bringing me a Valentine.

Whoever is this lady fair?

Whose love denies my greying hair?

Accumulating years are nought,

When cupid has his bow string taut.

CAPTAIN ROBERT BAILEY

So to this lady, sweet and fair,

Whose inspiration, love and care,

How lucky me, in all this time,

To get such loving Valentine.

How can such beauty bridge the years?

Eternal youth to me appears.

To be thy gift in all this time,

My wondrous, lovely Valentine.

49 VALENTINE TO THE DOCTOR'S RECEPTIONIST

This aching heart, with off spent sighs,

For one glance from those lovely eyes.

What silhouette of lissom line,

Could I but be thy Valentine?

How to control this beating heart,

Transfixed with love by Cupid's dart,

Or stop this pounding past description,

When she hands me my prescription.

And so sweet maid of lovely face,

How to describe that moving grace.

No less an angel sent from Heaven,

With surgery hours from six to seven

50 BIRTHDAY GREETINGS TO
MRS.THATCHER 13 OCTOBER 1983

O what a lovely morning now,

It's unlike any other.

When Margaret forgets her job

To be a wife and mother.

October thirteenth, special day:

When her birthday greeting wins

The warmest greeting of them all

From Dennis and the twins.

And unknown millions have their say,

Forget affairs of state.

How nice it is to be good looking

And only something eight.

May many happy birthdays come,

And who will wish you less.

Then good health through the coming years,

Long life and happiness.

Imaginary telegrams

From the Falkland Islanders to Mrs Thatcher

Thankful Birthday greeting to the Bantam from Grantham

From General Galtieri, in Argentina

To Merry Marguerite

Sweet English flower

Gentle as falcon

Or Hawk of the Tower

From Yuri Andropov

To walk with thee in England now,

Through lanes both wide and shady,

Sincerest wishes for this day

To England's iron Lady.

51 BIRTHDAY TRIBUTE TO MOTHERS BORN IN APRIL

Of all the months within the year

I think that April's best.

The dark days over, clocks move on

And nature does the rest.

The snowdrops, crocus, been and gone,

What wonders nature brings.

Where else a lovelier sight is these

Than daffodils in spring.

We love romantic fairy tales,

Prince, Princess and Elves.

How lucky can we families get,

A Princess to ourselves.

With boundless overflowing love

This princess born in spring,

Surrounds us with her loveliness,

What more can Nature bring?

So on this happiest of days,

And for the coming year

May all her future happiness

Be such that we might share.

52 A SEMI DETACHED HOUSE IN CLEVELEYS

Local Spiritualist obtained planning permission to use it as their church provided they used the back entrance. The lady next door objected, as she feared the spirits conjured up might wander into her house in mistake.

In Boggart Hole Clough, up in Pendle

The Boggart cum whum, feelin cowd.

He'd spent the day hauntin I Blegburn,

Ab gotten whun, feelin quite owd.

Ah'm getting too owd for this hauntin

Rheumatics, arthritis an aw.

Mu banshee wail fails o't top notes,

And ah now mi throat's gettin raw.

CAPTAIN ROBERT BAILEY

Ah've heard abeaut this Church in Cleveleys,

A little new place by the sea.

Won't do any harm, sh'd be cosy an warm,

It's just the place to suit me.

In Cleveleys ah meight get sum sunshine,

Away fro these hills, cowd an wet.

Them warm pebbly stones, meight wearm these owd bones,

It'll be the best place ah've had yet.

There's ony snag i this movin,

Ah'll never be left in the lurch.

Ah've not gotten plannin permission

To haunt thi new spiritual Church.

Whoever heard of a boggart,

At Lands End or ow John o'Groats,

Who has't ter get plannin permission

Before he could set out to haunt?

AROMA OF A REBEL

So let me advise aw young boggarts

Before thee goes practisin screams,

Consult with the Plannin Committee

Who'll tell thee what real hauntin means.

An if tha'rt goin ter Cleveleyes,

An tha' hasn't been theer befooer.

Remember, get plannin permission,

An then goo in throo't back door.

53 A WEDDING DAY

Today is a special wedding day

When everyone here gets pally, son.

You can't count the blessing

That marriage can bring.

There's no-one to take the tally, son.

A lot of give and a little take,

Then, there be no need, to rally, son

If things go amiss

A nice loving kiss

Will mean that you don't dilly, dally, son.

AROMA OF A REBEL

Surrounded today, by these lovely hearts,

Such mountains of wishes, no valley, son

What more can we say

On this special day

To David, and his lovely Alison.

54 PATRICIA'S BIRTHDAY 1982

A very special day today,

Good gracious, Heavens above.

We say "It's turned out nice again."

And all for our little love.

It seems so many years ago,

Mummy Ber goes, starry eyed,

Into that Blackpool nursing home

So happy, that she cried.

AROMA OF A REBEL

This ever constant miracle

Of babies born each day.

To us this lovely new born babe

Means love has come to stay.

So forty years have come and gone

Black hair has turned to grey.

To us, September twenty fourth

Means Little Love has stayed.

CAPTAIN ROBERT BAILEY

55 CHRISTENING OF SARAH BAILEY
AGED 5 MONTHS 31 OCTOBER 1982

October thirty first will be

Remembered for the way

Miss Sarah Bailey then made me

A Grandfather for a day.

This little pink clad baby

Just ate and slept all day.

Yet centred all attraction

As only baby's may.

AROMA OF A REBEL

The dark clothed surpliced Vicar

Long practised as his wont.

Relations gathered all around

The baby at the font.

Indifferently, Sarah,

Awakened with the dawn.

In spite of born good manners

Could not suppress a yawn.

And so, my lovely Sarah,

However much admired

There's only one New Zealand girl

That has this verse inspired.

Today's your five months birthday,

So tiny and alive.

Blood connections spans the years

Your five months, mine seventy five.

When you grow up, get curious

And wonder at your sires,

Your ancestry's in Wisbech

And Cambridge is the Sire,

So when you come to England,

And Wisbech's churchyard shows

That all your forbears came from there,

The Church has laid them low.

The tombstones' faded letters.

Tho' worth another look.

You'll find inside, the Vicar

Has kept a record book.

56 VALENTINE FOR PATRICIA

A lovely maiden, sweet of face

With Nature's form, rewarding grace.

But can I hope, in all this time,

To be thy unknown valentine.

To see that lovely shining smile,

Making all of life worth while.

To know the pleasure it can bring,

Like April flowers in the Spring.

Dark shiny eyes, and fair of hair,

How can I hope that you may care

To know there's love in every line

From me, thy would be Valentine.

57 VALENTINE TO SUE DAVIES OF THE EVENING GAZETTE

In *Bonny Mary of Argyll

There sings the lovely *mavis.

In the Gazette, a lovely love,

My true love, Susan Davies.

O wouldst that I could write like Burns

To tell thee how my poor heart yearns.

This aching heart, with offspent sighs,

For one glance from those lovely eyes.

And so sweet maid, please spare a thought

For the havoc thou hast wrought.

My poor heart feelings torn apart.

Pain, bitter sweet, from cupid's dart.

Such timeless beauty, of lovely face

This eye recording lissom grace.

Could I but be, in all the time,

Thy life long champion Valentine.

*Bonny Mary was Mary Campbell and was loved by Robert Burns but she died tragically young at about 23.

*mavis is a songthrush

58 VALENTINE IN RESPONSE TO VALENTINE CARDS

Alas my window peeping stare,

Revealing cards just standing there.

Had I the power these cards to move,

My rival for my ladies love.

Oh what a beautiful surprise

The postman shows my tired eyes.

That advance age, can blot out time,

When bringing me a Valentine.

CAPTAIN ROBERT BAILEY

Who ever are those ladies fair,

Whose love denies my greying hair?

That seventy years and more has wrought,

When Cupid has his bow string taut.

So to these ladies, sweet and fair,

Their inspiration, love and care.

How lucky me, in all the time

To get such loving Valentines.

59 DR. SMITH'S BARBARA

This aching heart, with offspent sighs

For one glance from those lovely eyes.

The pain from almost bursting heart,

Bitter sweet from Cupid's dart.

That lovely voice, so full of care,

Had I the courage, that I dare,

My one ambition, nectar sips

At those rose coloured, lovely lips.

CAPTAIN ROBERT BAILEY

Can I describe that lovely smile,

The lovely figure, Nature's style.

A nature sweet, skylark on wing

Or daffodils in early Spring.

Such lovely patience, natures own,

No wonder that my love has grown.

To see, perfection from afar,

My humble tribute to a star.

So Barbara, my love, my sweet,

My troubled heart is at thy feet.

Just give one sign in all this time

To thy most faithful Valentine.

60 TO DOREEN FEBRUARY 1983

The lovely lady, sweet Doreen,

Love's sweet perfection, always seen.

The lovely figure, Nature's line,

Could I but be thy Valentine?

This bleeding heart, with offspent sigh

For one glance from those lovely eyes.

To ease the pain in my poor heart,

Pain bitter sweet from Cupid's dart.

Alas the Goddess does not know

Love like mine, gives heartfelt glow.

That this poor mortal heart a pine

Could hope to be thy Valentine.

61 GILLIAN'S BIRTHDAY 1983

In February years ago,

This winter's weather mild,

There came to us from Barnsley

A lovely female child.

But what a day for her to choose

Born on the 29th of Feb.

A birthday only each four years,

How tangled is life's web.

The Bible says three score and ten,

At six she's very wily.

I've reckoned that her seventieth year

Two thousand two hundred and fifty.

But what a lovely day today

For us to welcome Gill.

Lovely baby now grown up.

Who else could fill Phil's bill?

Reluctant winter sunshine

Is brightened on this day.

Like crocus pushing through the snow

For Gillian's birthday.

And so our loving fondest wish

Is what we want to say.

The loveliest birthday of your life

With Returns of this happy day.

62 VISIT FROM THE HEALTH AUTHORITY

Wednesday April 10th 1985

Visit from Miss Kate Heald regarding chair lift

Today I had a visitor

Who made the day worthwhile.

She said from Health authority

Belied, by lovely smile.

With sympathetic nature

Officialdom must yield.

Her soft voice introduces herself

She said I am Miss Heald.

How oft to all with sickness bent

Across the doctor's filed.

To think that with Kate's aid we find

It's possible we're healed.

63 MARRIAGE OF KATE AND NIGEL

Whilst with me Miss Kate Heald explained she was getting married shortly to Nigel

O what a lovely day today

May twenty fifth, the date.

The day I've looked so forward to

When I marry lovely Kate.

And such a lovely month is May

With winter long at rest.

The apple trees are blossomed pink.

Dame Nature's at her best.

But all of nature's wonders pale,

Her beauty set aside.

Never such lovely radiance

Of Kate, my lovely bride.

The pear trees blossom dazzling white,

All nature now is stirred.

To welcome Preesall's lovely bride

Content, like nesting bird.

So to our future happiness

My heartfelt wish this date.

May I live ever after with

My sweet and lovely Kate.

64 MR AND MRS MUGRIDGE'S GOLDEN WEDDING

It started once upon a time

As all good stories do.

Young Arthur met this lovely girl

A fairy tale come true.

A lovely face and slim of form,

Young Arthur was impressed.

He didn't need his friends to say

That he had got the best.

And Phyllis seeing this young man,

Good looking, tall and straight.

CAPTAIN ROBERT BAILEY

Perhaps it was his dark moustache

That gave him added weight.

So now it's fifty years ago

When all their dreams came true.

A lovely life of wedded bliss

Experienced by few.

There is an old expression

Of Derby and his Joan.

When you've got five grandchildren

You seldom live alone.

As children came thought the years,

There's Colin, Hazel, Clive.

All bringing them their grandchildren,

Their dreams have come alive.

There's Laura, Sara, Leslie too

With Catherine and Charlotte.

Who'd dream that fifty years ago

How rich would be their lot?

What can we say who know them well

But send our love and kisses.

The still good looking Mr. M

And lovely looking Mrs.

May all their years, they have to come

Be happy, love filled, bright.

This be the wishes of us all

Who've gathered here tonight.

So let us toast this lovely pair,

We're all here with our wives.

To Arthur and his lovely bride

Who've brightened all our lives.

How lovely Phyllis was that day

When she saw Arthur's book.

She never knew till later on

That he could also cook.

65 MRS TEBBIT: STOKE MADEVILLE
APRIL 1985

Dear *Mrs Tebbit, happy morn,

A letter from the blue.

And from a perfect stranger

Not even known to you.

How soon the public memory fades

The Brighton bombs long past.

Our heartfelt wish for you today

Its ill effects won't last.

Those sleepless nights

You're lying there.

You think what can it mean?

If only I'd have stayed at home:

You think what might have been.

Why should I be the one that's hurt,

Of all the people there?

Now all's forgotten, except those

Who bring me loving care.

So when the dawn seems far away

And endless night stands still.

Remember you've our sympathy

We know you've got the will.

For all these months you've had to fight

Bad health, depressing mood.

Expressed in Churchill's famous words,

Such inner fortitude.

So never think that you're alone,

There's thousands more like me,

You've never met and never will

But wish recovery.

And so dear lady, here's good health,

And fortune without tears.

With all you loved ones, round about

For now and coming years.

So when the next convention comes

To Blackpool where you're from,

I'll get my wheelchair serviced so

I'll race you on the Prom.

Margaret Tebbit wife of Norman Tebbit (Lord Tebbit) was paralysed in the IRA bombing at the Grand Hotel in Brighton during the Conservative Party conference in 1984.

66 RACHEL'S BIRTHDAY NOVEMBER 1985

Birthday greetings to a lovely young lady named Rachel

Of all the months within the year

That Nature does adorn,

November 22nd is the day

A lovely child was born.

The lovely child of smiling face,

The figures slim, all moving grace.

Who cares if skies are overcast.

A treasured bundle born at last.

So to a young and lovely girl,

We hope that coming years

Will bring her happiness and love

And sunshine and no tears.

67 TO BRIAN AND JOAN 5 DECEMBER 1984

Today I'm feeling desolate,

This room is cold and drear,

Because we've had to wave them off

Our friends have gone from here.

I'm sitting in my easy chair,

Tis afternoon for tea.

Alas the settee's empty

Of vanished lovely knee.

So, please return in May or June

When Blackpool's at its best.

How lovely then to see you both

And set our minds at rest.

68 PATRICIA'S BIRTHDAY 1985

Remember, remember the fifth of November,

Gunpowder treason and plot.

We just remember a day in September,

The one day when we got the lot.

She started out as a very small child,

But my goodness, how she did grow.

How she loved to chatter so much,

It's one thing that we'll never know.

The only thing we've learned in this trouble and strife

There's dull days with clouds up above.

But one ray of sunshine that came in our life

Was brought by Patricia, our love.

So we just remember, this day in September,

A special day, all through the years.

How lucky we've been, a daughter supreme,

Who's brought us more sunshine than tears.

So this special day, we go on our way,

With blessings from all up above.

We're thrilled as we say and it all one way,

For Tricia, our own little love.

69 CHRISTMAS 1983 PATRICIA'S PRESENT: A COLOUR TV

I had a little TV set

And nothing would it show.

But a picture, black and white

In quite a healthy glow.

But now the Christmas fairies,

Who only work at night,

Mysteriously changed it

And set my room alight.

The pictures now in colour,

Brilliant rainbow bright.

Remote control brings comfort

Lying in bed at night.

And so to all good fairies,

Who once changed coins for teeth,

And now change television

For colour underneath.

To goblins, elves and fairies

Who live both far and near,

A lovely Merry Christmas

And colourful New Year.

70 PATRICIA LOVE 1984

My lovely lady, heart of grace,

My longing for thy lovely face.

My yearning heart, with love so fine,

Could I but be thy Valentine?

How to describe those dark brown eyes,

When my heart's filled with loving sighs.

This heart can't even rest awhile,

So oft disturbed by radiant smile.

What can I do to help me prove

This overpowering, joyous love?

Encompassing for all time

Thy secret loving Valentine.

And so sweet maid, please spare a thought

For this poor creature, overwrought.

Forever longing for all time,

Thy lifelong champion Valentine.

71 PA'S POTATO PIE-PERILS OF DIY

Two weeks ago when Mother was ill,

She asked Dad to mind us and Dad said "I will."

He got our meals ready and put us to bed.

But the first Sunday dinner, near killed us instead.

He brought in the pie to the table,

And sat there with proud smiling face.

If you had this served at the *Pembroke

You wouldn't have felt out of place.

Then we had to hide all our feelings

As Father plunged knife into crust.

The crust bounced away to the ceiling

And Father said "Well I'll be bust."

He put it back in the larder,

And then took a short running kick.

He stubbed his toe, and our sister Jo

Said, "I'll get my new hockey stick."

Then Mummy came in: solved the problem.

Our father saw just what she meant.

He'd forgotten to use her self raising.

He'd mixed some DIY cement.

Some one said, ask a policeman;

We all thought that this would be best.

He said "if I must remove all that crust

It will make me a bullet proof vest."

 *Pembroke is an up market Blackpool hotel.

72 TV REMOTE CONTROL

There must be thousands of housewives,

If we could just take a poll.

All of whom say, of that sorry day,

When they got a remote control.

Now Father sits there in his armchair,

The TV control close at hand.

Then right in the midst of a western,

I suddenly hear a brass band.

CAPTAIN ROBERT BAILEY

I listen to new pearls of wisdom

From Margaret to Anthony Benn.

Then suddenly snappy, when Dad's trigger happy,

There Attenborough's New Guinea hen.

I'll never forgive the inventor

Of this awful TV control.

I find it's far more insidious

Than Government's fact leaking mole.

What greater romance than a love scene

De Havilland and nice Errol Flynn.

Then click and the programme changes

We then get that Rubbishy Bin.

And so may I ask all you readers

How can I make this nuisance cease.

Think I'll settle down, with never a frown,

And watch a full programme in peace.

73 CHILD PROOF BOTTLES

This morning, I went to the chemist,

Although I didn't feel ill.

He gave me a new childproof bottle

Containing my arthritis pills.

The label it said, "please read instructions."

Which seemed very simple to me.

A little mark on the plastic,

And you turn the top round to the Vee.

When I returned from my shopping

I confess I felt out of place.

Unopened pills on the table,

And Father was red in the face.

Like most men he's not very patient,

You know how annoyed they can get.

He said "don't tell me about that mark Vee,

I've gone through the whole alphabet."

He got a screwdriver and hammer,

I knew he wouldn't be beat.

He looked high and low and then a quick blow

And the top came off all nice and neat.

I rang up the Doctor's reception,

He's got such a nice lovely lass.

I said, "Will I be ill, if I take a pill

Along with some fine broken glass?"

The moral of this little story

The chemist must pull up his socks.

I won't be ill, if I get my pill

In an old fashioned little round box.

74 TRIBUTE TO THE DOCTOR

A lovely man, so tall and fair,

Such elegant features, greying hair.

To seek his visit, my heart pines,

My secret love, my Valentine.

And when I see his car arrive

My fluttering heart, comes all alive.

My heart abounds, like an antelope,

At one glance at his stethoscope.

He looks at me, his glance perplexed,

I wonder what is coming next.

He says, "I cannot understand

Your fast heart beats like a military band."

75 GRANDMA'S NEW COOKER

First of all I must tell you,

Already, I'm three score and ten.

It's years since I had a new cooker,

The last one was Heaven knows when.

The oven control on this cooker

At three hundred and fully alive.

Whereas the knob on the old one

Went up to four seventy five.

CAPTAIN ROBERT BAILEY

The old one was Fahrenheit, Grandma.

The new one is marked Centigrade.

It's easy to make the conversion

Then you'll find that you've got it made.

You take the degrees on the cooker

And then multiply it by eight.

Divide it by five then add thirty two,

Then you will have Fahrenheit straight.

Remembering then all the old days,

When I was a young child at school.

The back of the exercise notebook

Examples of fractions and rules.

You saw all at once what a chain was,

It didn't mean long research.

It wasn't by chance, you saw at a glance,

How long was a rod, pole and perch.

But now with this metrification,

You multiply everything by ten.

Don't worry about yards or furlongs,

You're not going to see them again.

So why can't the makers of cookers

Make it easy for us on the job.

Inside the knob, Fahrenheit heating,

And Centigrade outside the knob.

76 FAKE TEETH

Sir John had travelled from London

To speak at the Workingmen's club.

Unfortunately his new dentures

Couldn't stand the dining car's grub.

To the Secretary he said "I'm sorry

I cannot speak without teeth."

The Secretary said, "do not worry

Just come to the office beneath."

AROMA OF A REBEL

"There's a man there called Jim'll fixit,

Who'll fix you up right away."

Sir John went down, emerged without frown,

With a top set, as bright as the day.

Then after the speeches were over,

Sir John called the Secretary aside.

"Congratulation to you and your dentist

I feel that my smile's a mile wide."

The Secretary said, "he's no dentist

Not even a dental inspector.

In his office beneath, he's got lots of teeth,

He's our local funeral director."

77 AN OLD LANCASHIRE JOKE

A fisherman went

A drowning worms.

Excuse me telling you

In such terms.

When a chap

With a face so glum

Looked over the wall of the Asylum.

Ha Ha Ha He He He.

"How many fish

Has ta' caught ?" said he.

"Never a bite,"

The man replied.

Said the lunatic,

"Come on inside."

78 29TH MAY 1977

We have a lovely daughter

But she's away just now.

She finds that North Wales calling

And this we must allow.

The house seems strangely empty

With everything in place.

It's always quite so tidy

Without that absent face.

Now Mummy Ber with feet up

Upon the new settee.

Say's, "I'll just do the bottles,"

Remember, only me."

And so more days are passing

With housework getting low.

One sandwich for breakfast,

One apple less and so.

79 JIM AND EMILY DECORATING

It's nice to have our friends to lunch

And see their friendly smile.

Now Emily joined Hilda and Jim

And says, "Is it worthwhile?

I left my little house at home

To have a holiday.

And now I've got an apron on,

It seems I'm here to stay.

I find I'm first assistant to

The decorator Jim.

I do the work, he sticks it   on,

I'll never alter him.

I've to measure every piece

And then put on the paste."

Jim stands there, all languid like,

Then says, "there is no haste.

We've all our life to decorate

Who care if fast or slow.

I must make sure that it looks nice

And everything just so.

In case the roll has been cut short

And I've to fit it in,

I'll do it better sobered up

Than when tanked up on gin."

Then Emily said, "I heard of these

They're working holiday.

This holiday includes the work

Except there is no pay!"

80 MISS SINGLETON PRESTON PO

Tonight, I'd such a nice surprise

To hear a lovely voice

Saying is that Mister Smith?

Of course I had no choice.

Except to say of course that's me

My grammar could be better.

I'd rather hear this lovely voice

Than get the *PO's letter.

It made me feel all young again

My suffering limbs got limber.

That husky dulcet, welcome voice

And what a lovely timbre.

AROMA OF A REBEL

I've heard about the PO girls

Especially from Preston.

Such lovely built up area

That your head can rest on.

The girls from Bristol can't compete

You've heard of Bristol city?

When you've seen the Preston girls

On Bristol have your pity.

In compliment, I must say this

Reception is so nice.

If I have got to be cut off

I wouldn't think but twice.

To telephone Preston PO

From Falls in Ingleton.

And if you have to send someone

Please send Miss Singleton

*PO Post Office

169

81 ODE TO MISS SINGLETON PRESTON PO JUNE 24TH 1977

My very dear Miss Singleton,

It makes my heart rejoice

To pick up my new telephone

And hear your lovely voice.

This time, I'll behave myself,

You put me in the mood.

A little bit of gentle verse

And never one word rude.

AROMA OF A REBEL

How nice to have your interest,

I'll see you when I can.

Now you've joined exclusively

The fan club with one fan.

I find it is so difficult

To write in virgin white.

I'm so much out of practise

The words won't come just right.

I thought you'd like to read aloud

My efforts for this week.

They're only good when topical

And interest at its peak.

And if the verse lifts tedium

At Preston *GPO,

It's very good for my moral

It'll help the old GPO.

*General Post Office

82 HARRY'S PAINTING PRESENT 1ST DECEMBER 1977

This morning post a big surprise

A postman's feeling shirty.

He said this parcel very wide

It's twenty nine by thirty.

The family gathered round agog

It must be a painting.

We can't undo it fast enough,

The girls are almost fainting.

AROMA OF A REBEL

Excitement rises, where's it from?

What do you think is in it?

Now don't get so excited girls,

You'll see it in a minute.

At last the wrappers off, unveiled,

A masterpiece by Harry.

Now proudly hanging at the shop

So passers-by will tarry.

Appreciating all the time

And careful preparation.

We sent to Harry, all our thanks,

As well as this citation.

So nice to come at Christmas time

Our greetings come with care,

To wish you all you wish yourselves

For Christmas and New Year.

83 ON GETTING OLD 18TH APRIL 1978

Ah, sorry day was March the tenth,

When my wife started counting

The whisky bottles in the bin

The rate at which they're mounting.

Now, I don't like the younger set

Whose shoes are always risky,

I answer calls and telephone

And sip a drop of whisky.

At seventy one, my days are done

With gambolling so frisky.

I sit at home with telephone

And sip a drop of whisky.

The callers for my daughter's flats

I answer them so briskly.

The Reverend Tomkins books his flat

I sit and sip my whisky.

I find it very difficult

Now getting stiff and old.

It must be a far right worse

To get much stiffer and cold.

84 TWENTY ONE YEARS OLD

Important day in every life

When babyhood is done.

A most important day in every life

And should bring lots of fun.

A birthday such a happy day

Beginning years not ends.

When everyone will wish you well,

A gathering of friends.

So here's a happy birthday,

May life bring lots of fun.

How nice to be good looking

And now only twenty one.

The most important day in life,

Apart from one at birth,

Is one that Philip now has reached.

It's called the twenty first.

85 WEDDING ANNIVERSAY 21 JULY 1989

How can one count the love that's gone

In forty years of marriage?

To lovely, gracious, Mummy Ber,

So beautiful, such carriage.

To such a youthful lovely girl,

Mouth corners turned with laughter.

I'm not embarrassed anymore

When she is called my daughter.

AROMA OF A REBEL

How can it be, that all these years,

She's figured fine, such beauty.

In spite of housework, cooking meals,

And not one sense of duty.

Such outpourings of love and you,

Who else, with love intense,

Could suffer all these sparks of life

And still retains such sense

How patient she, as model wife,

With normal tempered husband.

Such depths of patience hardly known

Throughout the breadth of England.

86 MY BIRTHDAY 7 JUNE 1978

It's nice to have a birthday

With lots of birthday cards.

Some of them are now so long

They're selling by the yard.

Old people start to reminisce,

Becoming quite a bore.

But there's a large card here today,

I think I've seen before.

87 FINE ON LIBRARY BOOKS 3 NOVEMBER 1979

May I offer a light hearted ditty

To the local library committee,

Who mulches the old timers,

The new seventy niners,

For a measly few bob in the kitty.

88 MEDIA NEWS OF PRINCE CHARLES AND LADY DIANA SPENCER

The nicest of our fairy tales,

Age old but ever new,

Are all about the handsome Prince,

And of his Princess too.

In older days, the Prince would roam,

His squire rode by his side,

And always he was questing for

A fair and lovely bride.

But now the Fairy Queen has ruled,

A fairy tale come true.

Our young and handsome Prince of Wales

Has found his princess too.

A lovely maid so sweet of face,

Demure of smile and shy,

Of gentle manner, lissom grace,

Has caught the Prince's eye

For Diana Spencer, nobly born,

No need of fairy tales.

The whole of Britain's wishing her

The new Princess of Wales.

89 TO DANIEL NOVEMBER 24TH

Today is rough and windy,

It's pouring down as well.

But lovely news has just come through

The birth of Daniel.

The world news is depressing,

Earthquakes and strikes as well.

But lighting the broadcast news,

The birth of Daniel

AROMA OF A REBEL

How proud the brand new Mother,

Father's in seventh Heaven.

A further world wide champion

Comes in at six pounds seven.

Congratulations, then, we send you.

We hope that all is well.

For Mother and new Father

And lovely Daniel.

90 CHRISTMAS 1980

Twas Christmas Eve in the *Potteries,

The night just was dreary and wet.

One of the Christmas cards sat up and said

I wonder how cold it will get.

I don't like to be in this junk shop,

There's nothing here we can do,

Surrounded by second hand cookers,

And here we are brand spanking new.

AROMA OF A REBEL

The LEC fridge now has told me,

He's much less than six months old,

And as fridges go with their freezer

He's better than new when it's cold.

So let's all have new Christmas greetings,

Good nature all over the land.

The Potteries goods are all useful:

Perhaps new or just second hand.

The Christmas card said this was helpful,

A Christmas flavour to hand.

And once they had been delivered

This made them all second hand.

*Potteries was a small shop selling second hand goods.

91 TO MRS ULLMAN WHO INTRODUCED
THE 18 PENCE RATE LEVY: MARCH 10
1982

I see Mrs Ullman's photo

And think what a lovely girl.

What classic nose, her eyes and mouth,

With hair that just the right curl.

We've all read of Queen Cleopatra

Who touched the asp to her lips.

Or even the lovelier Helen of Troy,

Whose face launched a thousand ships.

But neither can touch Mrs Ullman,

Whose beauty we can't denigrate.

She's just launched her first five thousand

SLIPS for non payment of rates.

92 REQUEST POEM ON FIRST ANNIVERSARY OF A HUSBAND'S DEATH

For twenty seven years we loved,

And now my love has gone.

For one a year of dark despair,

For him, earth's labours done.

But faith and time are easing pain,

I sometimes feel he's near.

Through faith, I know I'll meet again

The one I hold so dear.

93 MUMMY BER'S BIRTHDAY APRIL 3RD 1984

This lovely day is here again

We call it April third.

The daffodils are all in bloom,

We hear the Springtime bird.

They help us celebrate today

With one we love so dear.

Whose brought us so much happiness

For this and every year.

The cheerful face, the lovely smile,

The years have not diminished.

Impossible to count the years,

Her life time's work unfinished.

She never thinks about herself,

Her family always first.

Who takes so much for granted that

She always comes off worst.

Advancing years have taken toll,

She's never said she's clever.

But everyone who sees her now

Says beautiful as ever.

So for today our fondest wish,

No anniversary fears.

Long life and happiness from us

For this and other years.

So every morning when you wake,

Just think we love you too.

Your sacrifices are not spent

From Trish, and you know who.

94 DIVORCE OF A FRIEND 26 JUNE 1984

We read all sorts of funny things

In our Evening Gazette.

But Tuesday last was strangest,

The most peculiar yet.

Inside a special column there,

No advertising bills.

We saw a printed notice

Of our dear friends' Cockerills.

AROMA OF A REBEL

Now when you read divorces,

And this a special date.

Do you with years commiserate

Or split cork and celebrate.

Who brought the lovely flowers,

With greeting card beneath?

Was this a bouquet Muriel?

On Fred's going, a wreath?

CAPTAIN ROBERT BAILEY

95 WEDDING ANNIVERSAY 21 JULY 1984

After his wife fell from the top of stairs in their daughter's
bedroom.

For many years I've tried to write

And put my words to rhyme.

But this I find most difficult

To express thought to time.

What can I say my lovely wife,

To cover all the years,

From when you had your baby,

All sunshine no more fears.

196

AROMA OF A REBEL

That lovely would be mother.

The taxi driver swears

He'd never seen such radiance

In driving thirty years.

Apart from being beautiful,

With mannerism mild.

My lovely wife presented me

With Trish our lovely child.

To see her lovely face today,

Impossible it seems

That all these years have passed

Are actual not dreams.

You have to feel so young at heart,

Ignoring passing years.

To try a double somersault

When leaving Trisha's stairs.

Who could with such agility

Take off from Trisha's stairs.

Dislodge a TV desk and bed,

And never turn a hair.

It's just how young you think you feel,

Her philanthropic muses.

To make sure I didn't know

About her awful bruises.

How many memories conjured there

In all the time between.

For fifty years that lovely smile

As bright as sunshine's beam.

Who else has nature so possessed,

With all of nature's blessing.

That lovely form, the face so sweet,

No artificial blessings.

No word of mine can picture then

This lovely girl to see.

I'm thankful now, for all my life,

This wonder came to me.

So to this lady, age unknown,

Or gallantly suppressed.

I give my life long heartfelt thanks

To be so double blessed.

What other man can ever say,

When lifelong tales unfurl.

Whose been so lucky that he's got

Two young and lovely girls?

96 NICOLA'S FIRST BIRTHDAY AUGUST

How to describe those lovely eyes

Of such a vivid blue.

When Nicola upturns her face

And focuses on you.

Today is such a special day,

A special birthday too.

Nicola's reached the halfway stage

That goes from nought to two.

AROMA OF A REBEL

In case your mathematics fail

We'll help you on your way.

Today is most important cos'

She's one year old today.

Those lovely eyes, that lovely smile,

That only babe's possess.

The urge is irresistible

The baby to caress.

How effortless can babies' smile,

Ten thousand cupid's darts.

How innocent, how tenderly,

That captivates our heart.

To Bob then and to Barbara,

We send out heartfelt thanks.

For introducing Nicola

Into our love filled banks.

CAPTAIN ROBERT BAILEY

Our wishes on this special day

That babes do no wrong.

And in the many years to come,

She'll grow up big and strong.

So to the teenage Nicola,

The woman yet to be.

We all send all our fondest love

From grandparents in fee.

So twenty years from now

Who was this Mister B?

Adopted Grandfather you say,

Who sometimes spoke to me.

97 KAY MARY IN HOSPITAL

I often sing of Rose Marie,

Though some might spell it Kay.

Our warmest thoughts and get well card

Are all for you today.

So tarry not in Denbigh , love,

That's taking things too far.

Be on your telephone at home,

I'll wish you *"Bore da."

CAPTAIN ROBERT BAILEY

Of all the ladies on your ward

It's very plain to see.

That our loving thoughts are toward

Our lovely Kay Mary.

*Bore da is Welsh for good morning.

204

98 OUR DAUGHTER BECAME A VEGETARIAN 1984

Now Tricia won't eat little lambs.

She's now become a wary 'un.

To see a rabbit in its skin,

She says is quite a hairy 'un.

So meat and fowl are off her plate,

Her tastes are now sectarian.

She'll bounce from nuts to herbs and dates,

Since she went vegetarian.

So now my wife spends her time

Working like a Bavarian.

Getting cook books by the score

From our overworked librarian.

99 NEW NEIGHBOURS FEBRUARY 1985

Dear neighbours, you must find it strange,

Your furniture you must arrange.

What a turmoil you must have

When moving into this tree lined ave.

This note is just to welcome you,

So this won't feel so strange to you.

Not only will it break the ice,

You'll find your neighbours very nice.

If you need help of any kind,

Please don't feel shy, 'cos we don't mind.

Just come across the road and ask,

We'll help you with the smallest task.

We'll baby sit for your night out.

Once introduced you'll bear me out.

How difficult it always seems

To find the house of all your dreams.

And just to keep the records straight,

We live at number one two eight.

We'd like to meet you when you've time.

You'll be our latest Valentine.

100 MUMMY BER'S BIRTHDAY APRIL 3RD 1985

Of all the months within the year

We think that April's best.

With spring time lovely promised joys,

It outstrips all the rest.

The snowdrops now have been and gone

Replaced by crocus bright.

All natures bursting into bud,

Young shoots all seek the light.

But April's special day, the third,

Announced by spring and happy bird.

The lovely girl child born for us

Such beauty undisturbed.

The apple tree in pale pink buds,

The blackbird's song is high.

O what a lovely day today

When April third is night.

This lovely lady smiling face,

Figure slim and moving grace.

Now born to augment Nature's smile,

And April's wonders all worthwhile.

So lovely lady on this day,

Our heartfelt love is on its way.

You come to us as sunshine bright

And lovely April must be right.

101 ATTENDING A FUNERAL

When Dad saw the funeral notice,

Reading his Evening Gazette.

About an old friend of long standing,

He read it again, with regret.

He went to the funeral service

Arriving just a bit late.

Now that he's well over seventy,

He's very slow "getting agate."

There's one thing about congregations,

And this is a bit of old news.

Perhaps they're shy, but I don't know why,

They always fill up the back pews.

Dad walked down the aisle, walking stick style,

Feeling his nerves on the go.

His eyes left and right, no seat was in sight

Until he had reached the front row.

There's one thing that Dad's very proud of

His lovely high pitched tenor voice.

He'll start very low, to a high tremolo,

When the Parson says, "come and rejoice."

He loves to sing on the high notes

The Old Rugged Cross without frown.

You should hear him sing when he hits the high ceiling,

"Before his trophies laid down."

Now Dad had just seen the dentist,

At his age a bit of a goose.

The dentist was thinking, his gums were shrinking,

That left the top set feeling loose.

So when Dad hit the last high note,

He opened his mouth full and wide.

He saw a pink blur, fly through the air,

His top set had gone for a ride.

They slid on the lid of the coffin,

The Vicar's reaction was swift.

The time he took to "take off" in

Was faster than our war time blitz.

The number of times playing cricket,

His best work was done in the slips.

He fielded the teeth, the coffin beneath,

With the Rugged Cross still on Dad's lips.

The people all there didn't notice,

The Vicar gave Dad his teeth back.

All they heard him say was, "Now let us pray

For the family of friend Joseph Black."

102 POSTSCRIPT BY HIS DAUGHTER

My Father struggled in later years in his walking. In spite of this, he opened a second hand shop in his 70's. He went out buying and shifted many of the fridge's cookers and freezers himself.

He spent a lot of time sitting in his chair where he delighted to read the local daily newspaper. Oft times these would result in a poem or letter to the Editor. Some were printed some were not. Whether you agree with his viewpoint or not at least he did something about what he read.

He also liked to get what he asked for so when he went into a shop and asked for a pound of meat he wouldn't let the girl get away with a pound and one ounce. He caused consternation to one young lady shop assistant on this issue but he got his pound of flesh. He promptly went next door into the greengrocers and took the young lady a bunch of flowers.

Which reminds me – he would often buy flowers for my Mother and put them in unusual places such as the bath.

103 OTHER PRODUCTS

Look at www.pesha.com for other Pesha products such as:-

"Adventures of a Rebel" by Captain Robert Bailey. "Adventures of a Rebel" is an autobiography of Captain Robert Bailey. He was born at the beginning of the last Century in Bolton, Lancashire, England. There are five main sections. The first covers the Music Hall where his Father was a professional comedian. The second covers his adventures with boats on the Thames including being shipwrecked. The third is when he was conscripted during Second World War but volunteered to serve in the Indian Army and tells how he came to be on All India Radio. The fourth covers his caravanning adventures particularly in Spain. The fifth covers his dabbling as a property developer in Eire.

"Trouble down the Tunnel" by Pesha (Captain Robert Bailey's daughter) Andy Appleyard's nightmare begins when his parent's marriage crumbles and they separate.

Court, Welfare Workers, Auntie Mary and terrorists are all involved.

Andy's parents don't seem to grasp the impact on their eight year old son but pursue their own agenda.

A fast paced exciting, wholesome, adventure story for the whole family. Both youngsters and grown ups alike will grow to love Andy and his friends and be thrilled by their escapades.

This is the first book in the Andy Appleyard series.

"Access to Children Course" on DVD by Pesha (Pat Bailey) who spent most of her 40 years at the Bar working in the Family Court as an Advocate. She shares with you what she has learned in a 4 volume integrated course. The DVD volumes of the Course are interlinked so it is helpful to buy all the volumes and watch them in order.

This Course is about you and your children or grandchildren and gives ideas and information to help you see them and keep in touch.

"Being with your children or grandchildren brings a deep contentment which compares with no other experience. It is my heartfelt desire this Access to Children Course will enable you to enjoy this contentment once again,"

You will be surprised how easy it is to follow this Access to Children Course which is packed full of tips, secrets and strategies which hopefully will help you in your struggle to get access to your children or grandchildren. The Access to Children Course is in four volumes each volume of about an hour.

After sharing only one of her tips at a Grandparent's meeting more than 25% reported success at the next meeting.

You will learn the best ways to get access to your children: possibly without a lawyer or going to Court. If you have go to Court you will learn what to do if you haven't a lawyer. If you have a lawyer you will learn how to make the best use of your lawyer and their costly time. You will learn how to make the best use of the Court.

You will discover getting access to your children usually has very little to do with the law. This makes the Access to Children Course internationally useful.

"My experience has been as an Advocate both in the Family Court and in high profile fraud cases and judging Employment cases. I have a law degree and postgraduate qualifications. I was Head of a Barristers Chambers for 9 years. But none of this will compare to the achievement of helping you gain access to your children and grandchildren." Pesha

Bringing out her first DVD album **"Hymns of Heaven and Comfort" Album One** at 70 and with an MRI scan saying "highly suspicious of endometrial cancer," Pesha has Heaven and Comfort firmly in her mind. Thoughtfully and deeply heartfelt she shares these lovely old fashioned hymns with you. She hopes they will bring encouragement and comfort. Videos accompany Pesha's sensitive singing and words on screen enable you to sing along. There is a CD and MP3 version.

ABOUT CAPTAIN ROBERT BAILEY

Captain Robert Bailey was born in Bolton in Lancashire in 1907. He was the penultimate child in a family of six children. He was a warm generous man who also wanted to help people. His home was full of singing and knew all the words to many, many of the old songs.

He was talented in many different ways including figure iceskating, riding on the wall of death, private pilot licence and could walk on his hands until he was about fifty.

He died twenty fourth of February 1986.

Look at www.pesha.com for more details.

www.ingramcontent.com/pod-product-compliance
Lightning Source LLC
Chambersburg PA
CBHW051954090426
42741CB00008B/1388